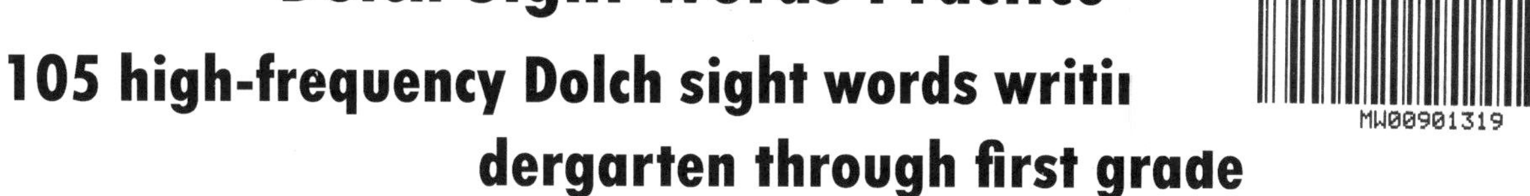

Dolch Sight Words Practice

105 high-frequency Dolch sight words writi[illegible] [illegible]dergarten through first grade

Write And Learn Sight Words Series. Volume 1

Printed by CreateSpace, An Amazon.com Company

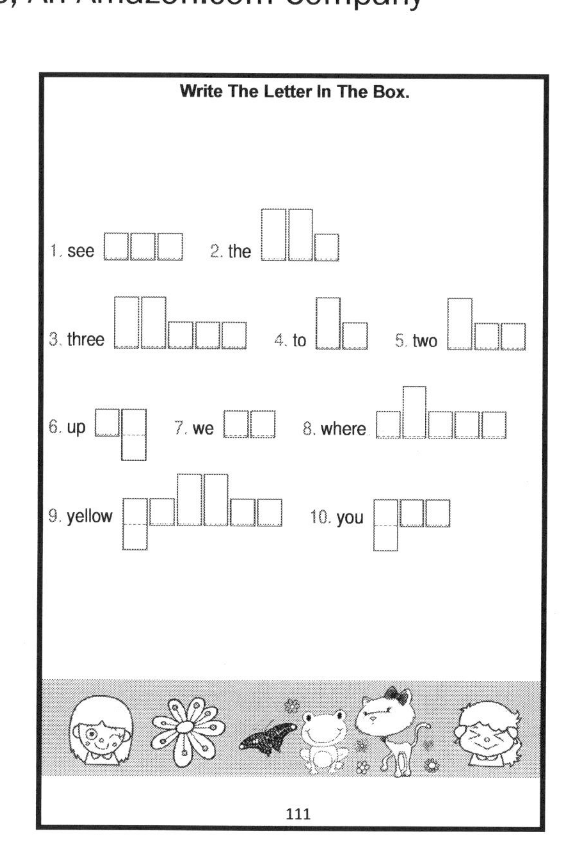

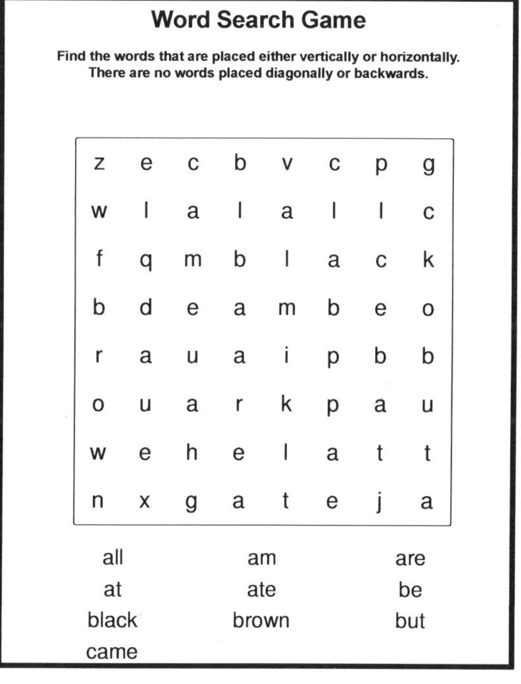

In This Write And Learn Series, You Will Find:

- **105 Dolch sight words**
- **105 pages of writing practice worksheets**
- **Write The Letter In The Box worksheets**
- **14 x Word Search Games**
- **2 x Maze for extra fun!**

Specially Designed For Pre-kindergarten Through First Grade

Contents

a

a a a

This is a dog.

and

and and and

My dad <u>and</u> I played catch.

away

away away away

The bird flew <u>away</u>.

big

big big big

This truck is **big**.

blue

blue blue blue

The sky is blue.

can

can can can

I <u>**can**</u> **kick a ball.**

come

come come come

Can you <u>come</u> here?

down

down down down

Put <u>down</u> your pen.

find

find find find

Did you find the cat?

for

This present is <u>for</u> you.

funny

funny funny funny

I can tell a <u>funny</u> joke.

go

go go go

I need to go to the toilet.

help

help help help

Can you <u>help</u> your friend?

here

here here here

I am **here**.

I

I am 5 years old.

in

in in in

You can come in now.

is

is is is

He is my brother.

it

it it it

I like <u>it</u> very much.

jump

jump jump jump

I can <u>jump</u> really high.

little

little little little

I have a <u>little</u> sister.

look

look look look

I <u>look</u> up and saw a plane.

make

make make make

I can **make** a paper plane.

me

me me me

This toy belongs to <u>me</u>.

my

my my my

He is <u>my</u> good friend.

not

not not not

I am not feeling well today.

one

one one one

I can eat <u>one</u> big hamburger.

play

play play play

Can you play with me?

red

red red red

My shirt is <u>red</u>.

run

run run run

Can we run together?

said

said said said

He **said** I am a clever boy.

see

see see see

Did you <u>see</u> my daddy?

the

the the the

Can you open <u>the</u> door?

three

three three three

There are <u>three</u> eggs in the basket.

to

to to to

Can I go <u>to</u> the mall today?

two

two two two

I have **two** ears.

up

up up up

I ran <u>up</u> the hill.

we

we we we

<u>We</u> like to eat candies.

where

where where where

<u>Where</u> are we going today?

yellow

yellow yellow yellow

The lemon is <u>yellow</u>.

you

you you you

I will play ball with <u>you</u>.

Kindergarten (52 words)

all

all all all

I ate all the cookies in the jar.

am

am am am

I <u>am</u> good at playing basketball.

are

are are are

Where <u>are</u> the apples?

at

Can we meet <u>at</u> the toy shop?

ate

ate ate ate

He <u>ate</u> his lunch late.

be

be be be

Do not <u>be</u> late for school.

black

black black black

This cat is **black**.

brown

brown brown brown

That is a <u>brown</u> bear.

but

but but but

I ate my lunch, but I am still hungry.

came

came came came

My grandmother came to my house.

did

did did did

She did well in her test.

do

do do do

Can you <u>do</u> the dishes?

eat

eat eat eat

What did you <u>eat</u> for dinner?

four

four four four

A chair has <u>four</u> legs.

get

Can you get me a drink?

good

good good good

This tastes very <u>good</u>.

have

have have have

I <u>have</u> a new watch.

he

he he he

<u>He</u> is from my hometown.

into

into into into

I walked <u>into</u> the supermarket.

like

like like like

Do you <u>like</u> your new shoes?

must

must must must

I **must** go now, my mum is waiting.

new

new new new

He is wearing a <u>new</u> hat.

no

no no no

<u>No</u>, I don't want to go to the zoo.

now

now now now

The movie will start <u>now</u>.

on

on on on

He sat <u>on</u> a chair.

our

our our our

Miss Nancy is our teacher.

out

out out out

He took <u>out</u> a cat from his bag.

please

please please please

<u>Please</u> give me back my book.

pretty

pretty pretty pretty

She is a <u>pretty</u> lady.

ran

ran ran ran

My dog ran away.

ride

ride ride ride

I want to ride on a horse.

saw

saw saw saw

He <u>saw</u> a rat.

say

say say say

Can you say that again?

she

she she she

<u>She</u> is my sister.

so

so so so

I am <u>so</u> cold.

soon

soon soon soon

It is going to rain soon.

that

that that that

Is <u>that</u> a cat on the tree?

there

Can you put your hat there?

they

they they they

They went to the mall together.

this

this this this

Is <u>this</u> yours?

too

too too too

This shirt is <u>too</u> big.

under

under under under

There is a rabbit under the tree.

want

want want want

I <u>want</u> to eat ice cream.

was

was was was

It **was** raining in the morning.

well

well well well

My mum is not feeling **well**.

went

went went went

I <u>went</u> to see the doctor yesterday.

what

what what what

<u>What</u> is the color of this shirt?

white

white white white

The cloud in the sky is <u>white</u>.

who

who who who

<u>Who</u> took my sandwich?

will

will will will

I <u>will</u> be late for school.

with

with with with

Can you play <u>with</u> me?

yes

yes yes yes

<u>Yes</u>, I like to have a cookie.

apple

apple apple apple

Here is an apple for you.

baby

baby baby baby

The baby is crying.

back

back back back

There is an ant on your back.

ball

ball ball ball

Throw me the <u>ball</u>.

bear

bear bear bear

Did you see a <u>bear</u> at the zoo?

bed

bed bed bed

What time do you go to <u>bed</u>?

bird

bird bird bird

Is that a yellow <u>bird</u> on the tree?

birthday

birthday birthday

birthday

This Sunday is my **birthday**.

boat

boat boat boat

That is a big <u>boat</u>.

box

box box box

Can you put your toy into the <u>box</u>?

boy

boy boy boy

Sam is a boy.

bread

bread bread bread

I like to put butter on my bread.

brother

brother brother brother

Tom is my **brother**.

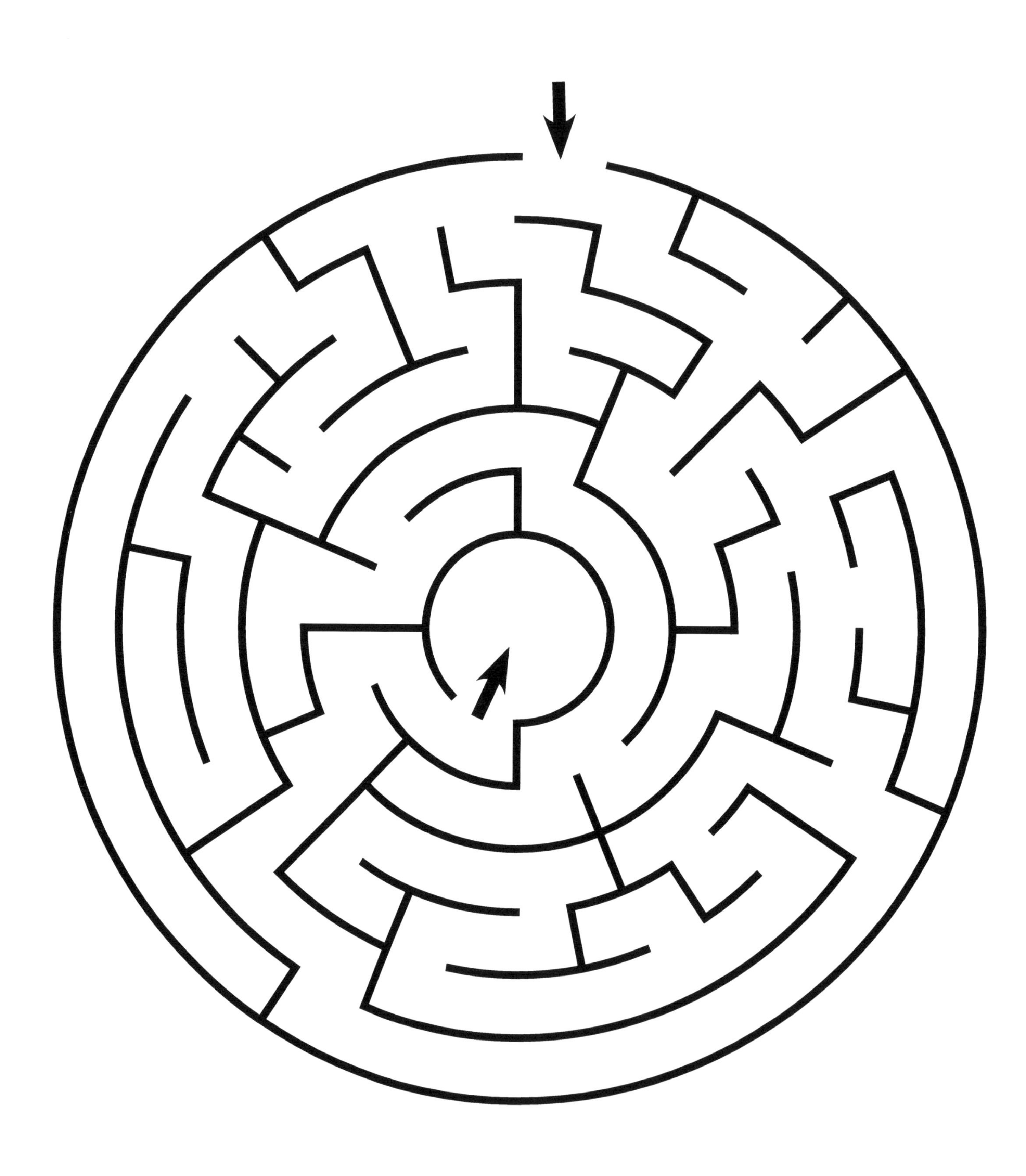

Write The Letter In The Box.

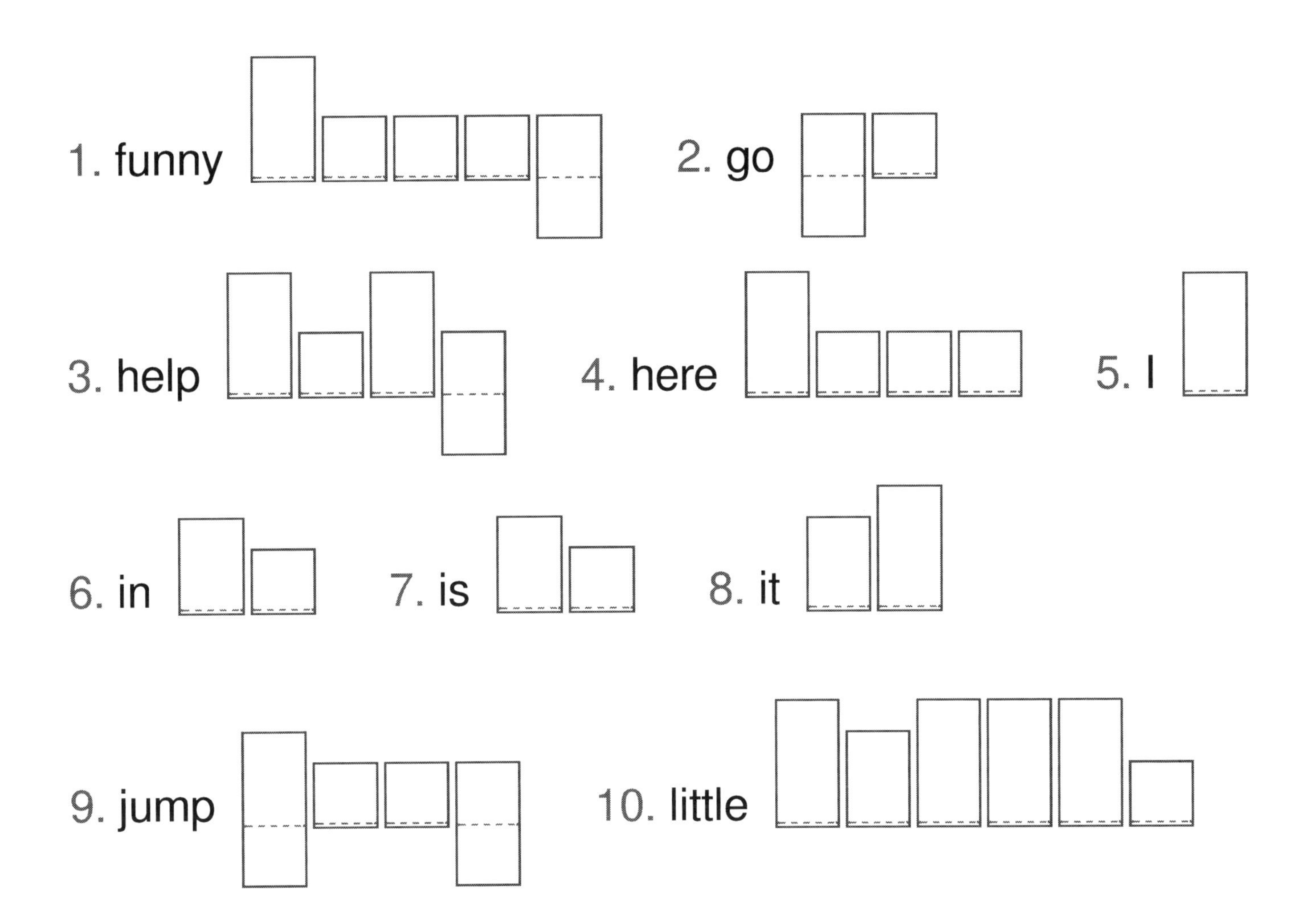

Write The Letter In The Box.

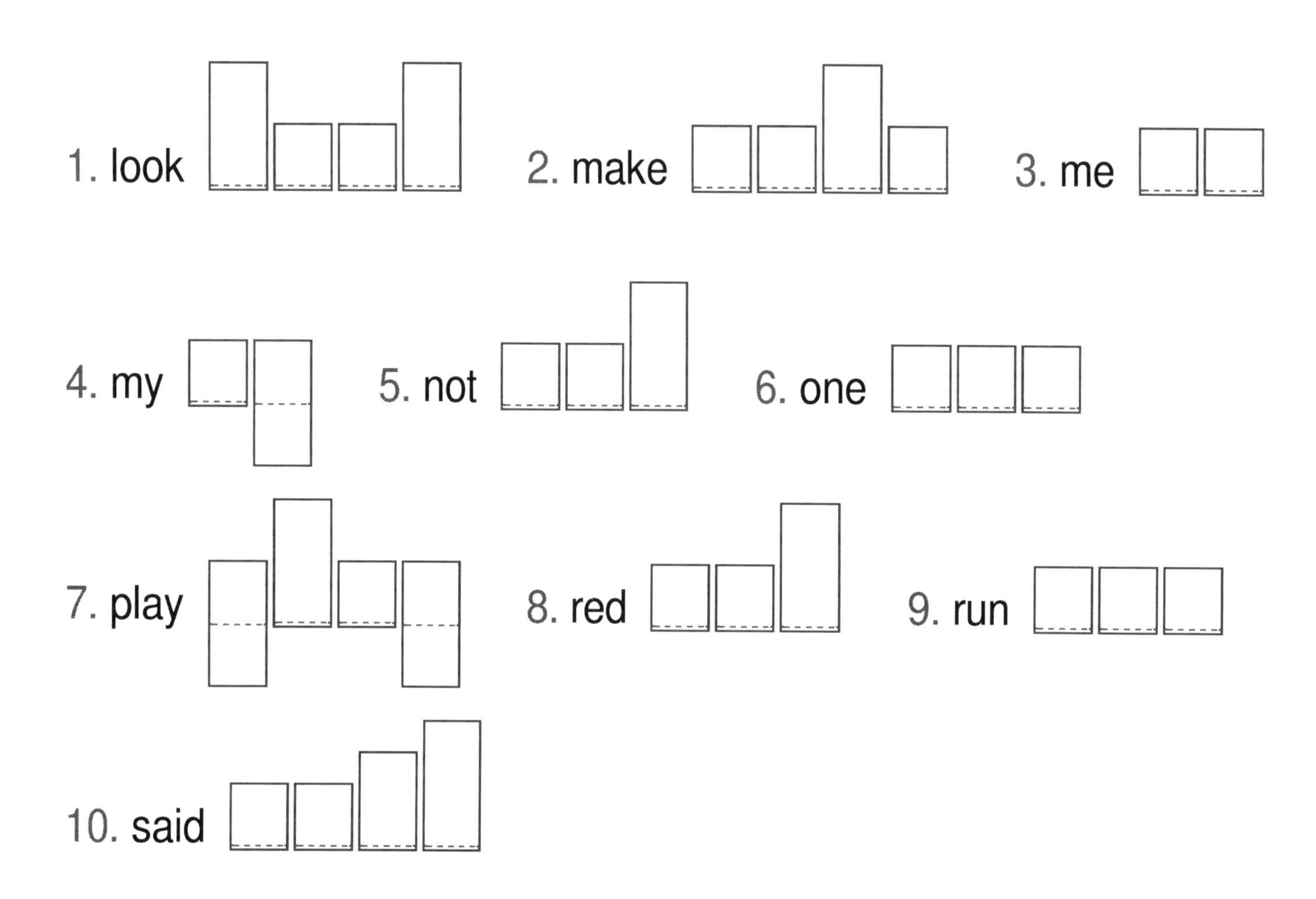

Write The Letter In The Box.

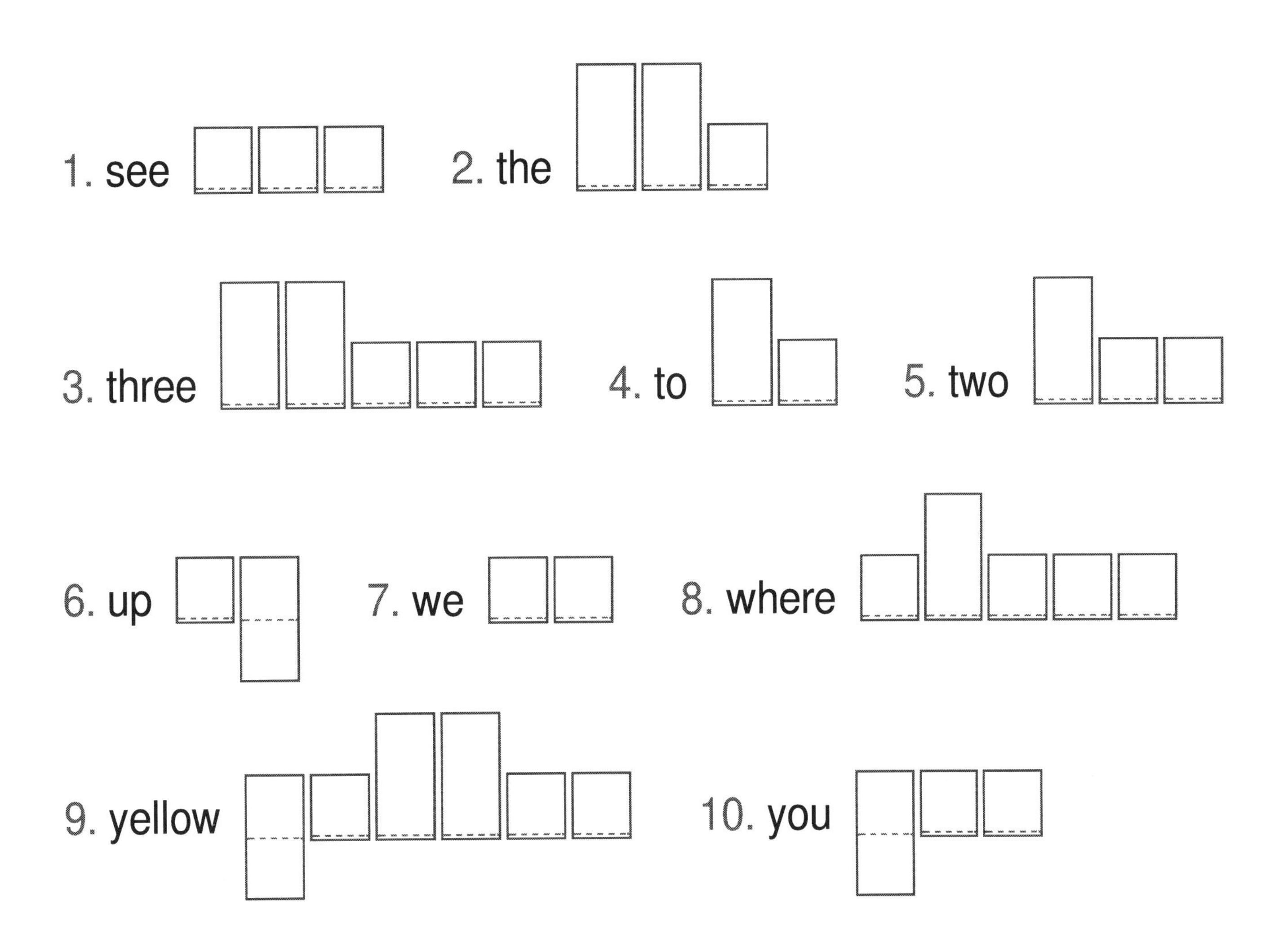

Write The Letter In The Box.

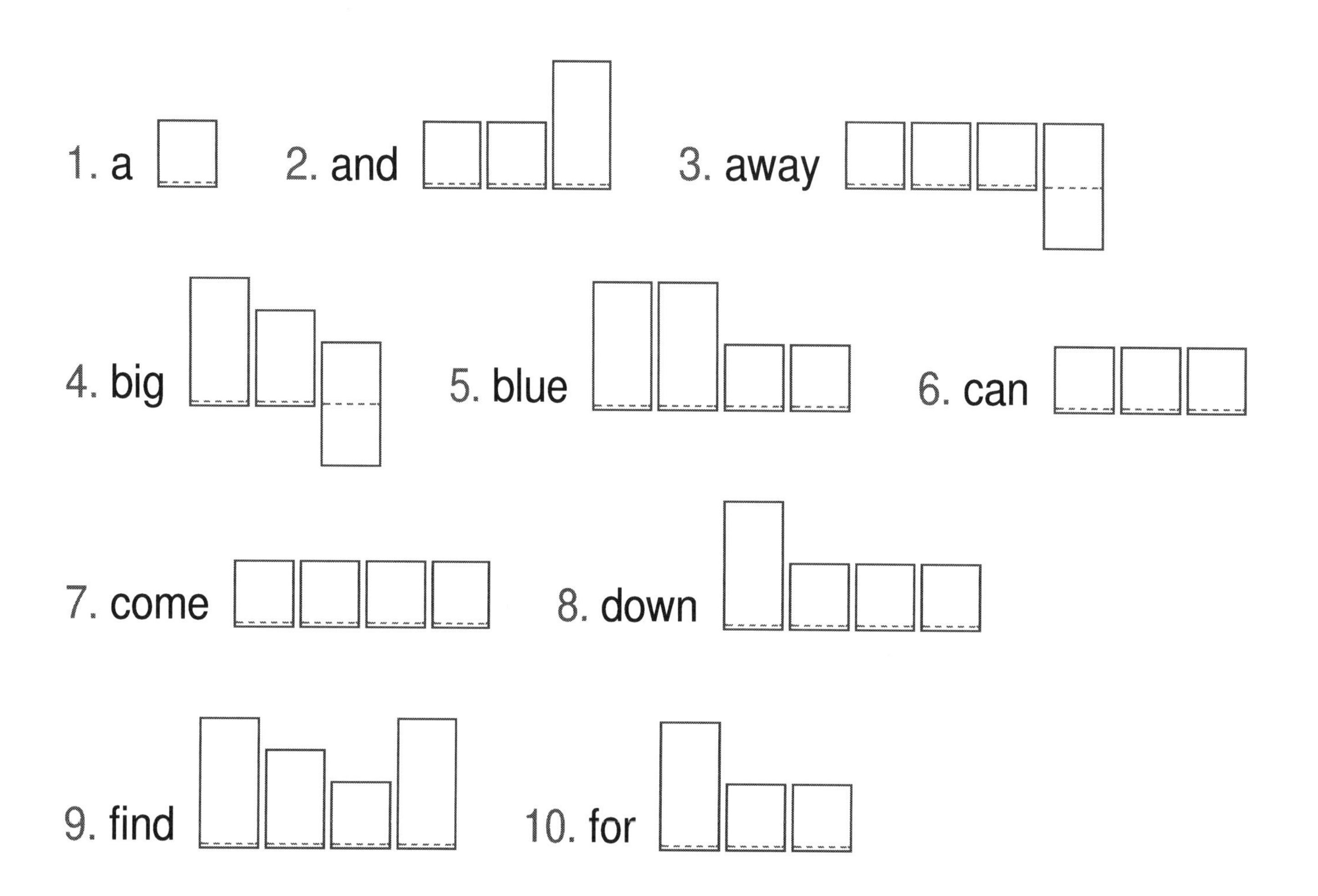

1. a
2. and
3. away
4. big
5. blue
6. can
7. come
8. down
9. find
10. for

Write The Letter In The Box.

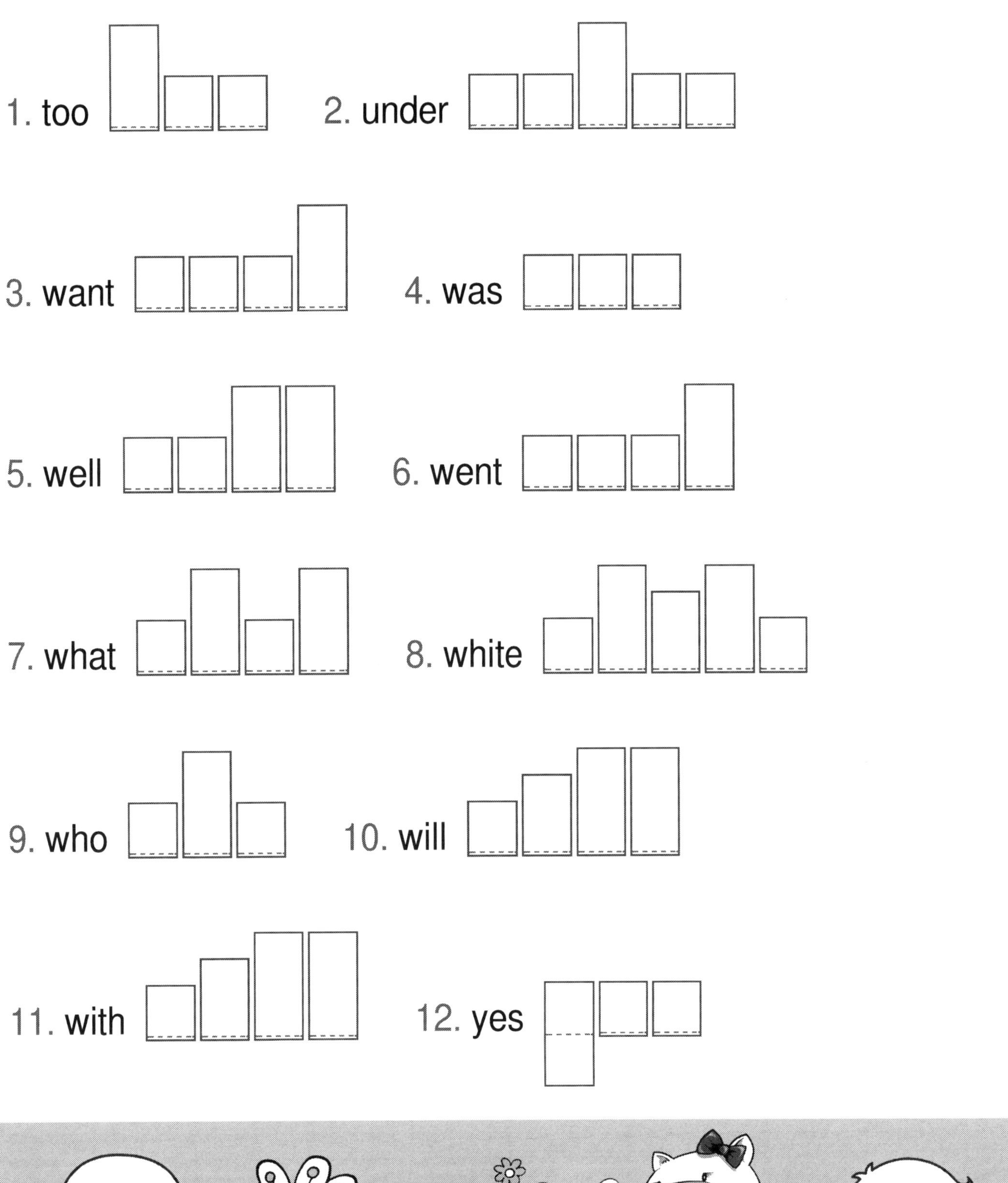

Write The Letter In The Box.

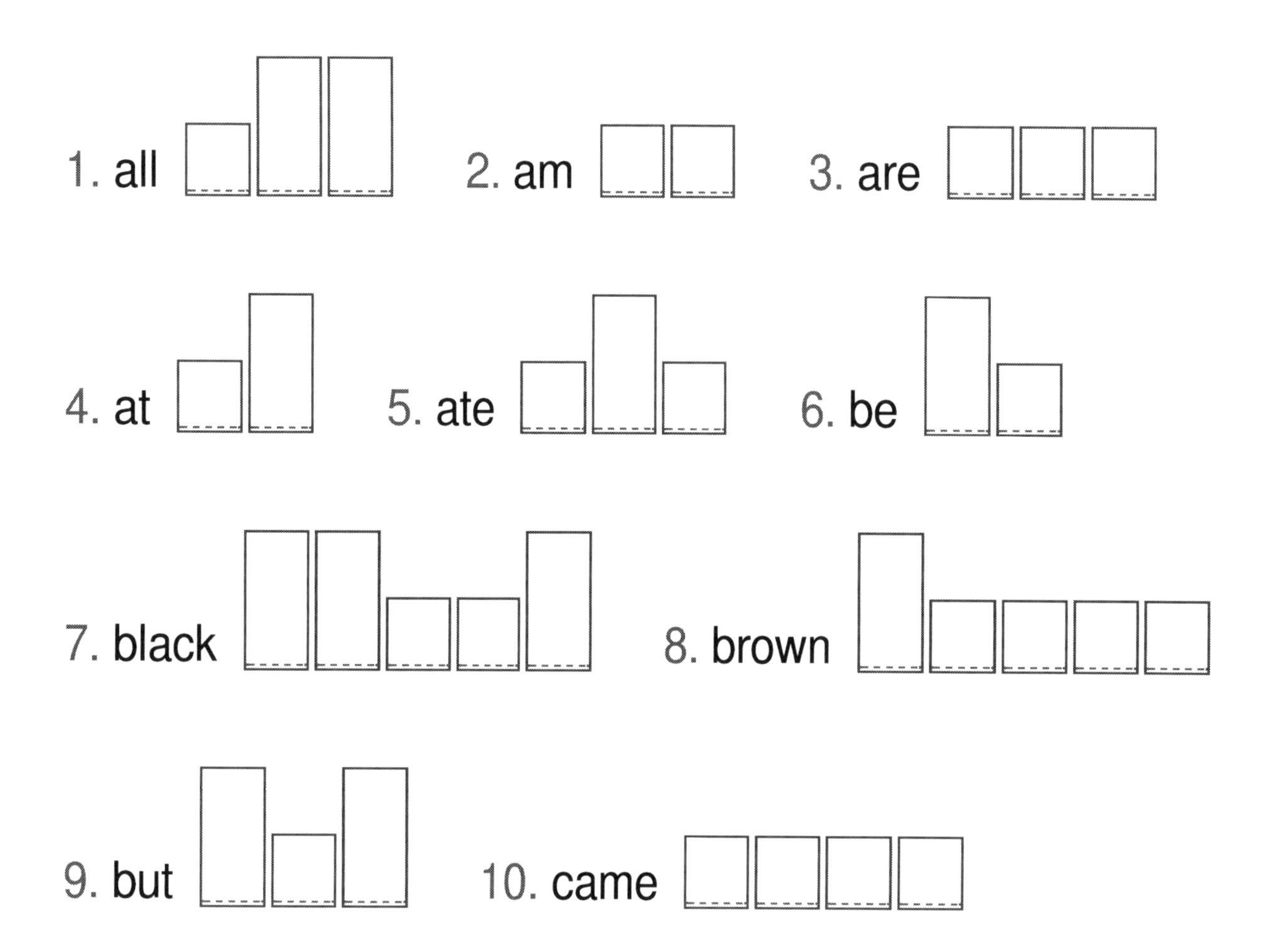

Write The Letter In The Box.

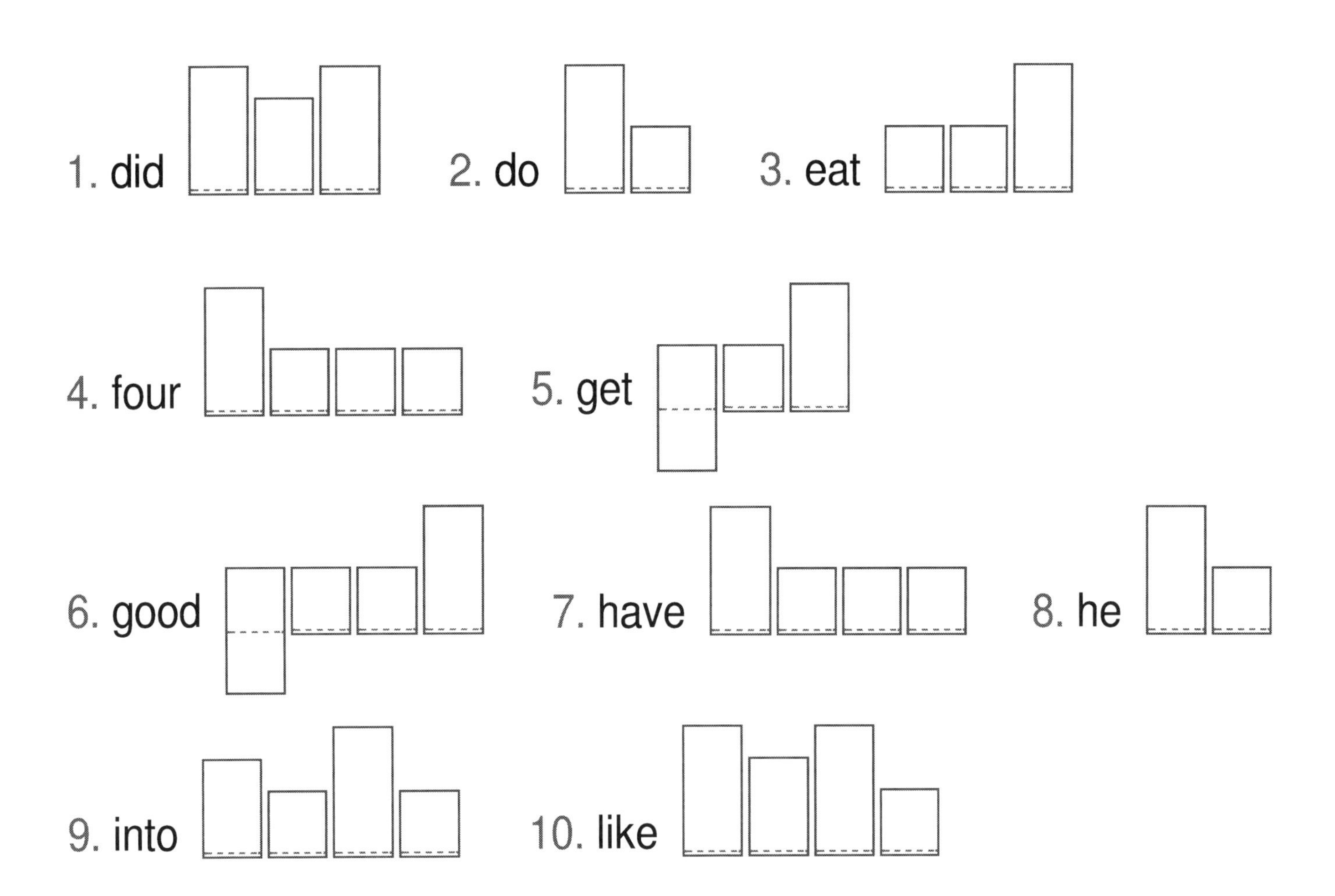

Write The Letter In The Box.

1. must
2. new
3. no
4. now
5. on
6. our
7. out
8. please
9. pretty
10. ran

Write The Letter In The Box.

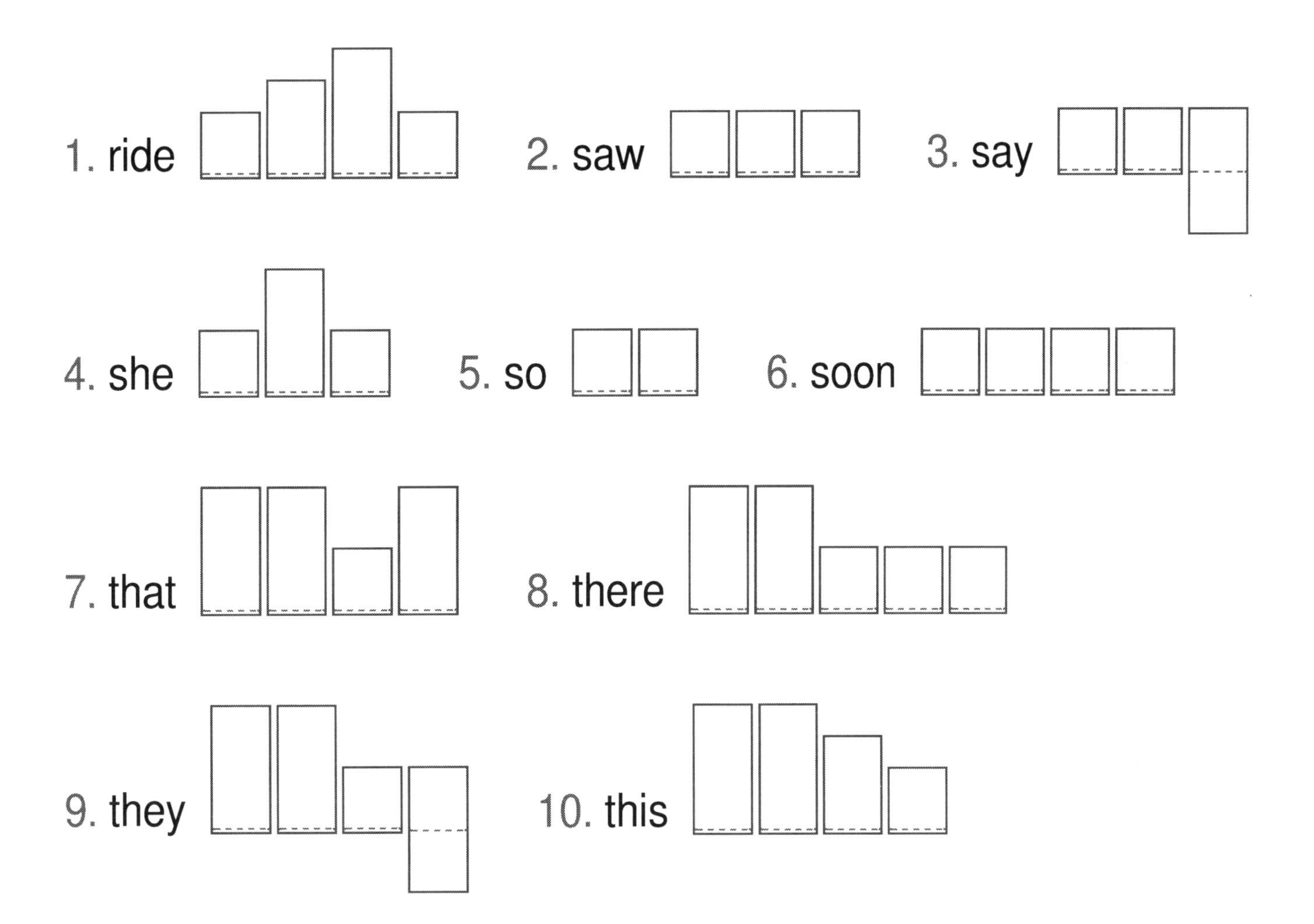

Word Search Game

Find the words that are placed either vertically or horizontally. There are no words placed diagonally or backwards.

b	f	i	z	g	f	m	w
u	y	a	k	j	k	c	c
k	u	b	d	m	i	w	g
p	s	n	o	t	k	z	o
l	x	v	b	r	a	v	q
a	h	z	r	e	d	f	g
y	b	r	p	o	f	b	p
t	r	f	j	o	n	e	t

not one play
red

Word Search Game

Find the words that are placed either vertically or horizontally. There are no words placed diagonally or backwards.

c	o	v	s	e	e	x	e
g	d	l	s	a	i	d	t
r	d	x	r	d	g	f	y
u	y	t	h	e	b	a	t
n	p	y	c	t	v	m	h
t	y	f	b	d	z	f	k
a	p	i	p	p	p	l	k
q	k	y	z	y	n	z	y

run said see
the

Word Search Game

Find the words that are placed either vertically or horizontally.
There are no words placed diagonally or backwards.

h	n	f	w	s	y	k	o
a	b	h	a	n	d	b	k
b	d	n	l	o	k	u	s
n	n	b	i	g	i	g	b
v	c	l	j	a	y	d	l
b	q	j	y	w	z	j	g
b	v	c	w	a	w	n	x
o	l	t	g	y	o	u	q

a　　and　　away

big

Word Search Game

Find the words that are placed either vertically or horizontally.
There are no words placed diagonally or backwards.

k	z	y	s	u	i	g	p
j	k	c	o	m	e	w	b
i	e	f	k	p	j	d	j
d	c	d	o	w	n	q	z
k	p	t	h	b	l	u	e
w	e	c	j	f	d	j	t
s	k	a	n	s	r	d	l
s	k	n	x	b	z	s	i

blue can come
down

Word Search Game

Find the words that are placed either vertically or horizontally.
There are no words placed diagonally or backwards.

z	a	z	b	f	z	e	e
v	a	f	o	r	v	x	f
k	j	n	f	i	r	w	u
o	s	q	i	f	f	p	n
d	u	a	n	z	f	o	n
w	m	u	d	q	b	u	y
w	y	h	g	l	v	l	e
g	o	j	u	k	j	t	n

find   for   funny

go

Word Search Game

Find the words that are placed either vertically or horizontally.
There are no words placed diagonally or backwards.

i	j	x	d	b	w	j	h
f	h	e	r	e	e	q	e
i	c	i	v	r	g	d	l
r	s	c	i	n	y	q	p
u	s	g	x	b	c	y	n
q	z	z	s	c	b	o	l
t	u	x	i	m	k	v	f
q	t	z	r	s	g	d	m

help here in

Word Search Game

Find the words that are placed either vertically or horizontally. There are no words placed diagonally or backwards.

m	u	o	g	b	c	u	b
z	r	w	e	k	w	h	n
d	z	s	m	i	s	t	r
c	l	i	t	t	l	e	n
q	j	a	u	f	g	x	c
r	u	m	b	r	v	n	c
s	m	d	o	g	k	n	z
i	p	o	e	v	z	i	t

is

it

jump

little

Word Search Game

Find the words that are placed either vertically or horizontally.
There are no words placed diagonally or backwards.

h	s	t	w	r	m	v	t
k	t	w	o	v	w	u	h
r	q	t	k	j	p	h	a
n	m	o	u	p	h	x	n
j	i	f	v	k	g	i	f
k	f	h	e	d	c	m	u
h	v	r	t	h	r	e	e
h	t	m	p	o	d	j	u

three   to   two

up

Word Search Game

Find the words that are placed either vertically or horizontally.
There are no words placed diagonally or backwards.

d	l	h	y	g	j	z	b
y	o	k	k	i	n	h	y
t	g	w	m	y	j	j	e
l	j	b	w	h	z	n	l
y	s	c	e	r	s	i	l
k	d	c	x	b	g	n	o
c	h	w	h	e	r	e	w
y	y	o	u	q	d	x	l

we where yellow
you

Word Search Game

Find the words that are placed either vertically or horizontally. There are no words placed diagonally or backwards.

z	e	c	b	v	c	p	g
w	l	a	l	a	l	l	c
f	q	m	b	l	a	c	k
b	d	e	a	m	b	e	o
r	a	u	a	i	p	b	b
o	u	a	r	k	p	a	u
w	e	h	e	l	a	t	t
n	x	g	a	t	e	j	a

all	am	are
at	ate	be
black	brown	but
came		

Word Search Game

**Find the words that are placed either vertically or horizontally.
There are no words placed diagonally or backwards.**

x	m	f	o	u	r	j	t
h	o	g	o	o	d	f	h
j	t	u	d	c	w	l	a
d	o	i	i	u	n	f	v
h	s	n	d	e	r	k	e
b	y	t	h	a	g	h	q
u	h	o	n	t	e	g	q
l	i	k	e	t	t	h	e

did	do	eat
four	get	good
have	he	into
like		

Word Search Game

Find the words that are placed either vertically or horizontally. There are no words placed diagonally or backwards.

g	j	z	g	n	e	w	i
g	h	o	g	h	a	k	a
v	j	n	m	u	s	t	y
q	p	r	e	t	t	y	y
p	l	e	a	s	e	m	d
h	o	g	f	q	n	p	n
t	u	r	a	n	o	l	o
p	r	v	o	u	t	r	w

must
new
no
now
on
our
out
please
pretty
ran

Word Search Game

Find the words that are placed either vertically or horizontally. There are no words placed diagonally or backwards.

y	s	h	e	t	s	a	w
t	b	i	y	h	s	e	f
h	t	d	t	e	s	v	s
e	s	o	h	y	b	w	o
r	n	y	i	y	u	t	o
e	i	c	s	u	s	h	n
r	i	d	e	w	a	a	f
m	h	t	o	o	y	t	e

ride	saw	say
she	so	soon
that	there	they
this	too	

Word Search Game

Find the words that are placed either vertically or horizontally.
There are no words placed diagonally or backwards.

a	w	i	t	h	r	w	y
w	h	i	t	e	y	a	w
f	x	d	h	v	x	n	i
g	u	n	d	e	r	t	l
w	y	w	x	y	l	c	l
e	e	h	h	p	w	a	s
l	s	a	w	h	o	c	d
l	n	t	w	e	n	t	p

under	want	was
well	went	what
white	who	will
with	yes	

Solutions To Maze

Solutions To Word Search

Puzzle 1

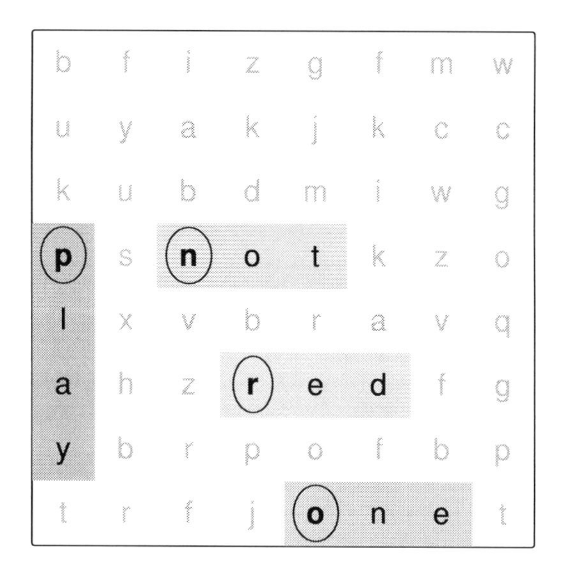

Puzzle 2

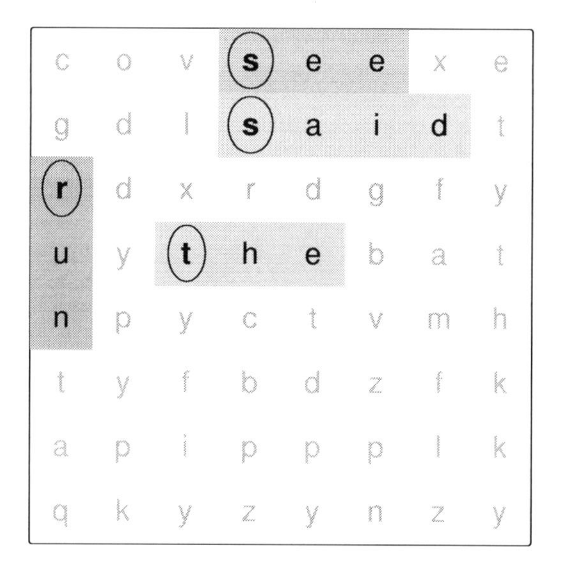

Puzzle 3

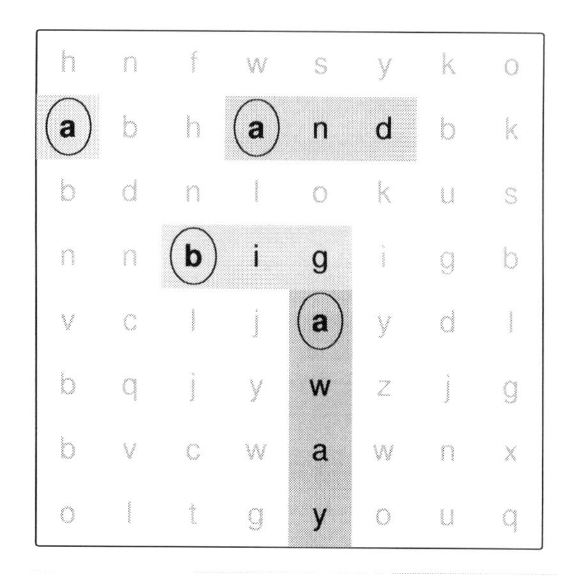

Puzzle 4

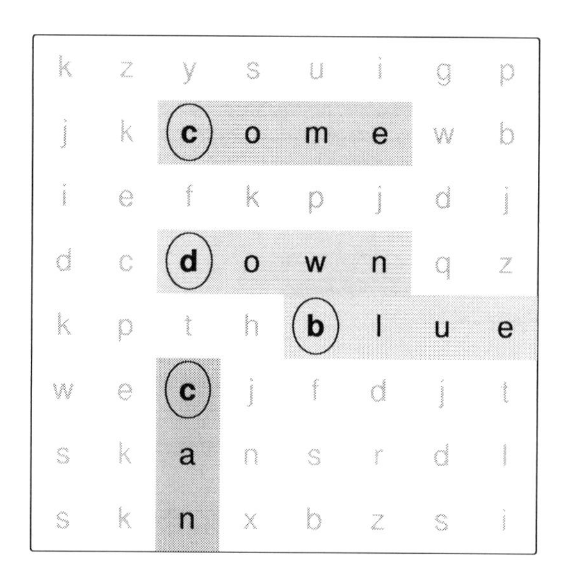

Solutions To Word Search

Puzzle 5

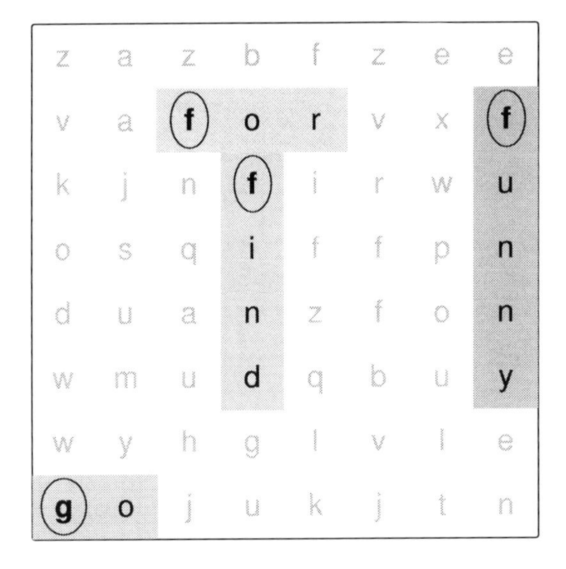

Puzzle 7

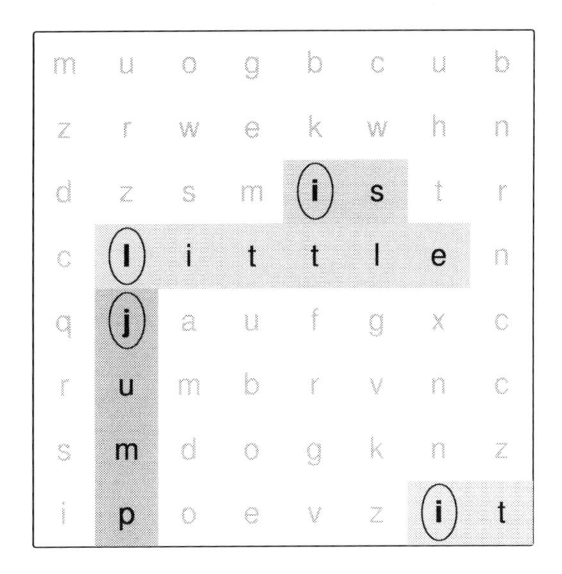

Puzzle 6

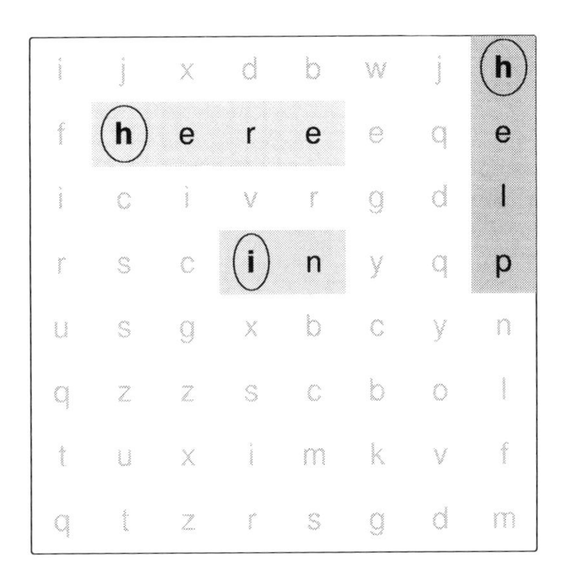

Puzzle 8

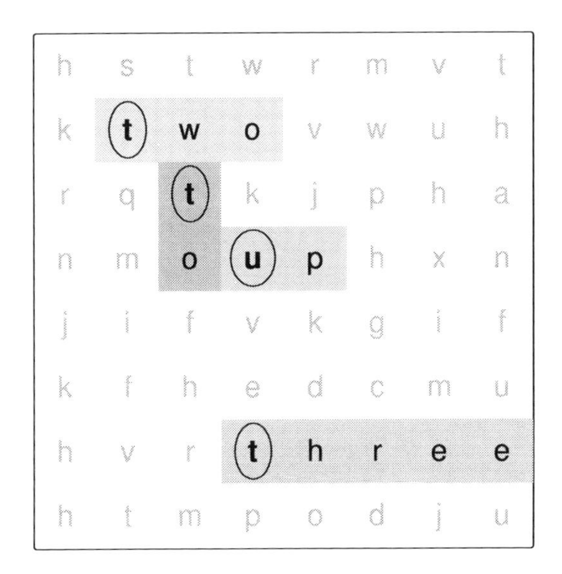

Solutions To Word Search

Puzzle 9

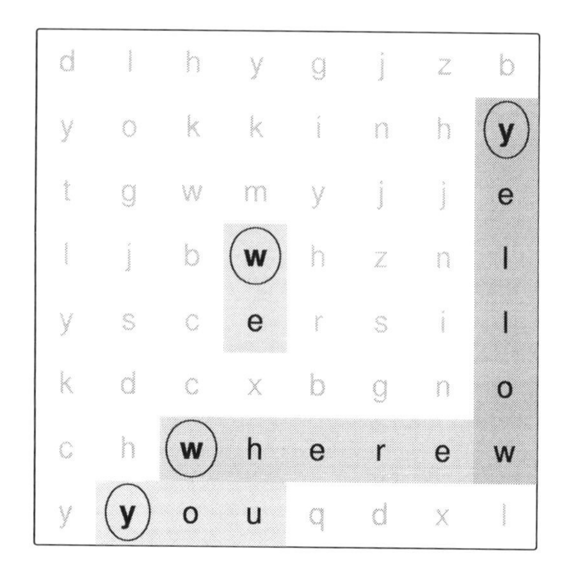

Puzzle 11

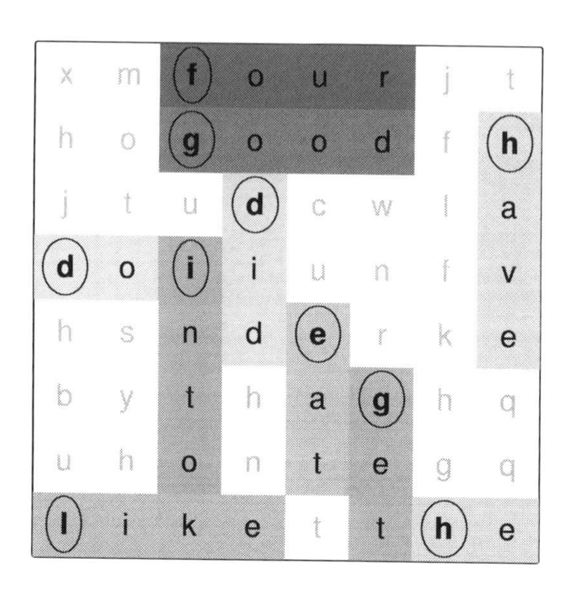

Puzzle 10

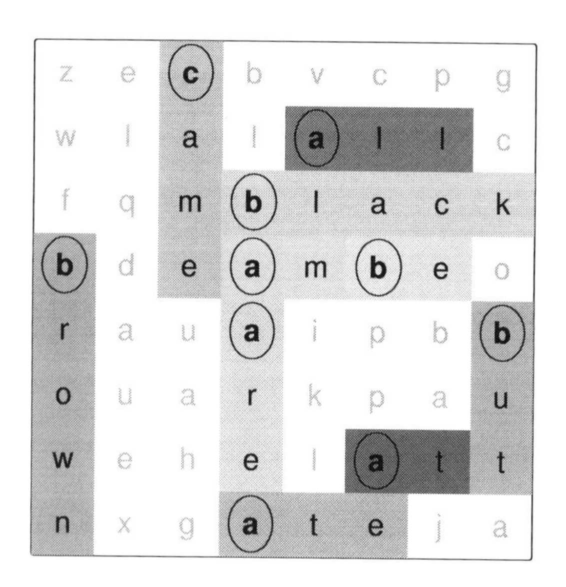

Puzzle 12

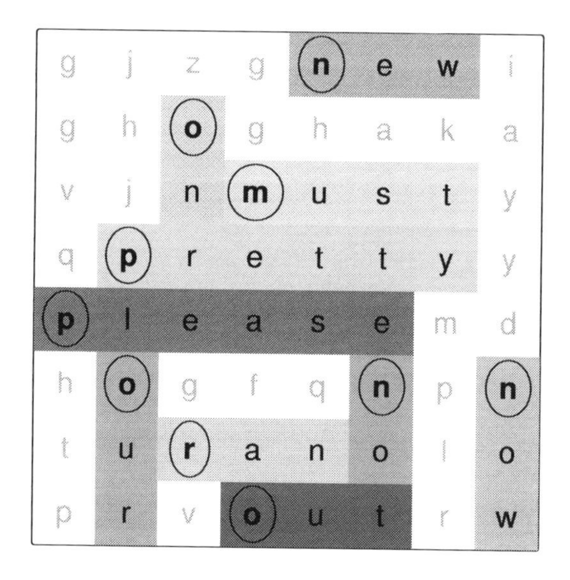

Solutions To Word Search

Puzzle 13

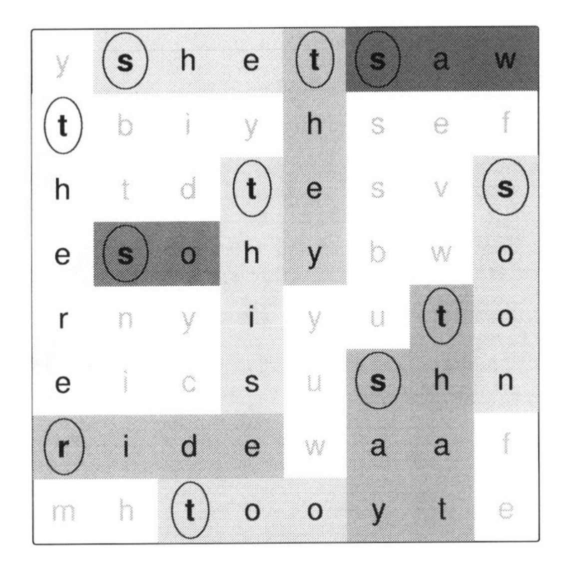

Puzzle 14

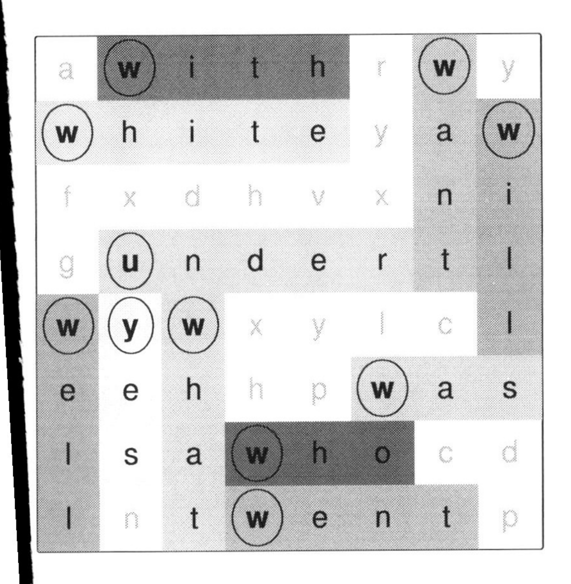

Made in the USA
San Bernardino, CA
21 August 2017